Alexander John Maisner

Ghosts of an English Playing Field
Recollections of the Future

<<<< >>>>

Alexander John Maisner was born in Louth, England and now
lives with his wife and their cat in Siegburg, Germany.
This book is the first published collection of the many poems
he has penned over the years.

Alexander John Maisner

A poetry collection

Ghosts of an English Playing Field
Recollections of the Future

for my lovely Treasure

<<<< >>>>

Bibliografische Information der Deutschen Nationalbibliothek:
Die Deutsche Nationalbibliothek verzeichnet diese Publikation in der
Deutschen Nationalbibliografie; detaillierte bibliografische Daten sind

im Internet über http://dnb.dnb.de abrufbar.

© 2020 Alexander John Maisner

Herstellung und Verlag
BoD - Books on Demand Norderstedt

ISBN: 9783751981156

1. Auflage
Printed in Germany

<<<< >>>>

Look up at the sky
and wonder why
we are so far apart
rest assured
you are deep within
my heart

5

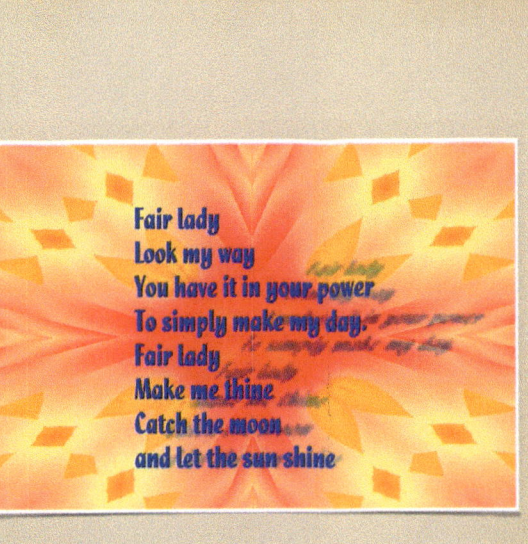

Fair lady
Look my way
You have it in your power
To simply make my day.
Fair lady
Make me thine
Catch the moon
and let the sun shine

6

you dance
like no other
floating on air
graceful dancer
subtle power
gentle sway
you dance
like no other
and I love you
to this day.

7

You fill the
night with light
and make a grey sky
blue
You turn a brown field green
the sunshine
comes from you.

Lay thee down
Beside me
Let me stroke your hair
Rest your head
Upon my shoulder
I kiss your eyes so fair
Seek comfort, warmth
Our worries
Let us share
And float away
On an endless dream.

9

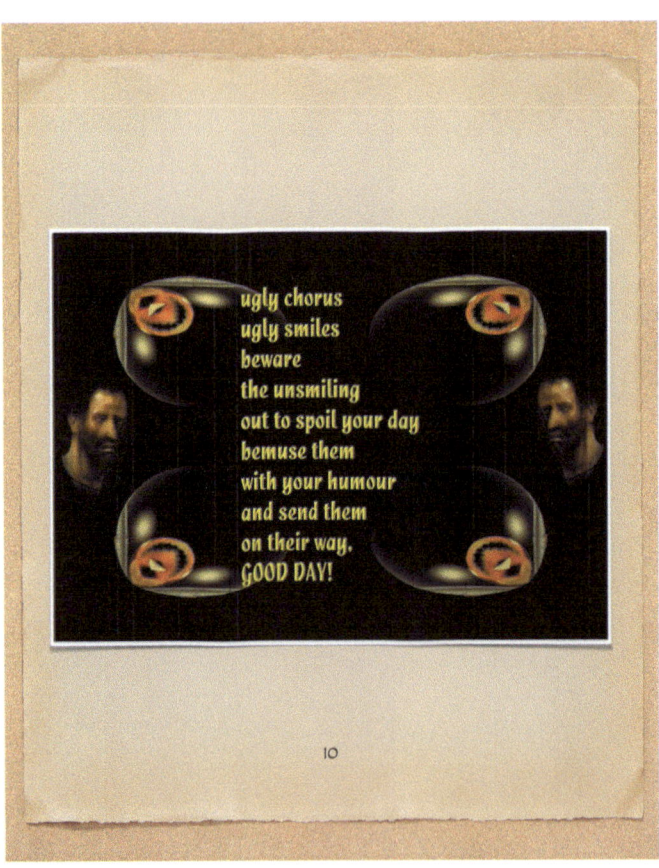

ugly chorus
ugly smiles
beware
the unsmiling
out to spoil your day
bemuse them
with your humour
and send them
on their way.
GOOD DAY!

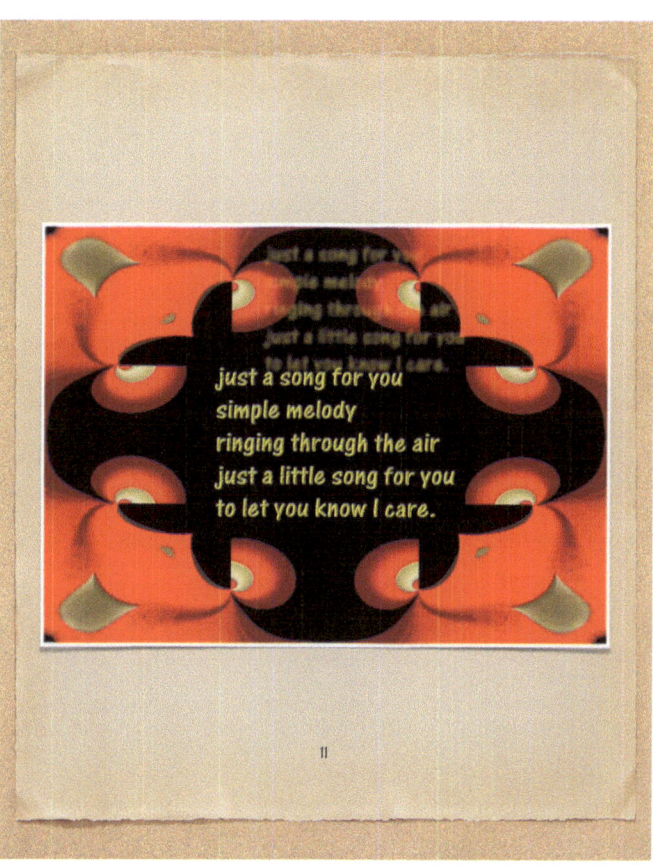

just a song for you
simple melody
ringing through the air
just a little song for you
to let you know I care.

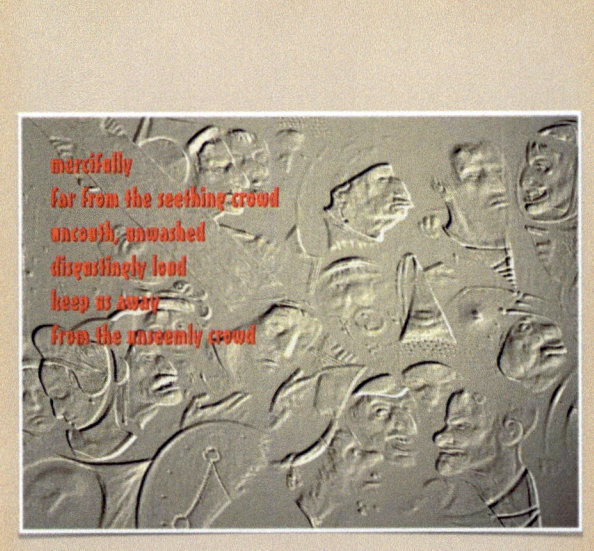

mercifully
far from the seething crowd
uncouth, unwashed
disgustingly loud
keep us away
from the unseemly crowd

12

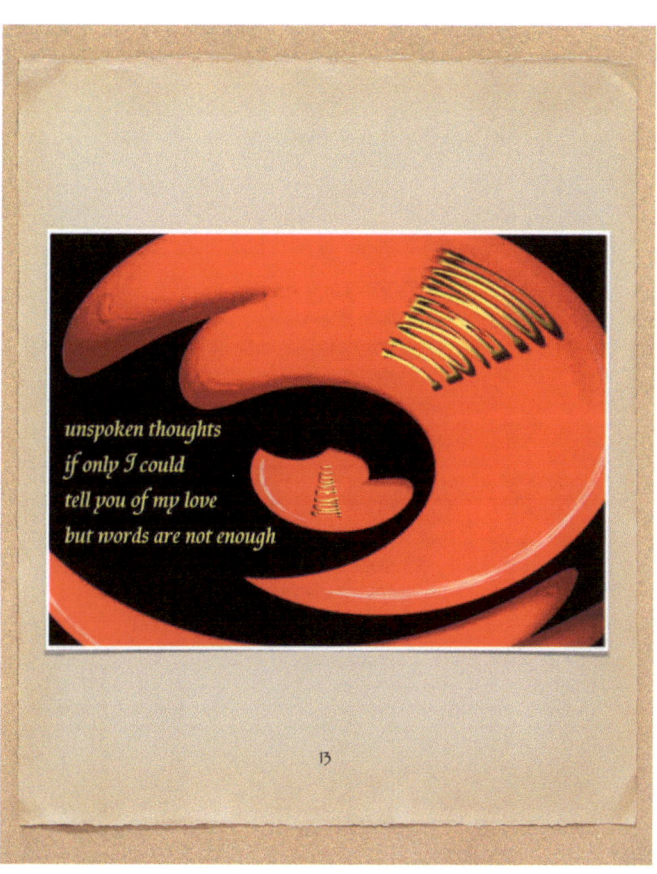

unspoken thoughts
if only I could
tell you of my love
but words are not enough

13

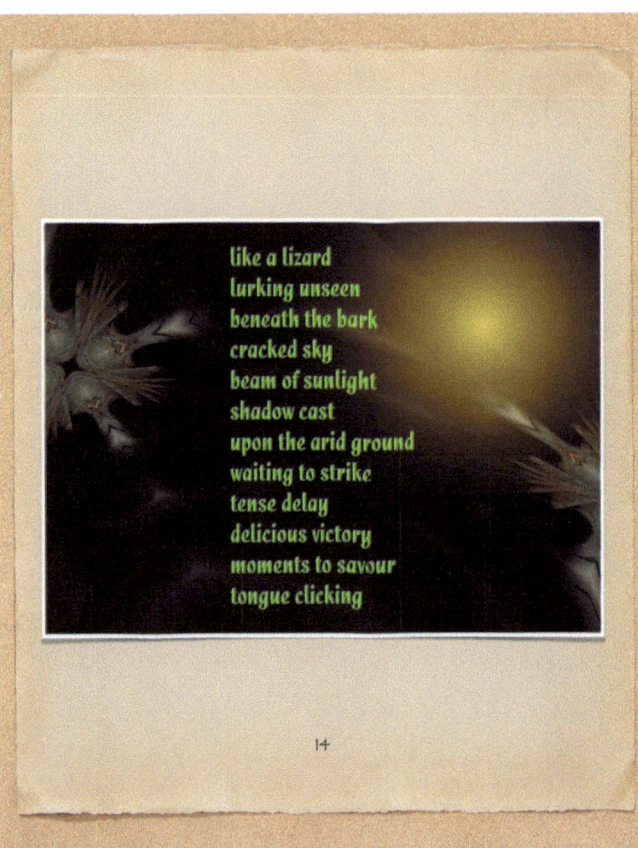

like a lizard
lurking unseen
beneath the bark
cracked sky
beam of sunlight
shadow cast
upon the arid ground
waiting to strike
tense delay
delicious victory
moments to savour
tongue clicking

14

Wise owl
watching on from lofty bough
impart your wisdom
gathered over years
looking down
upon the world
harmony of thought and deed
blending into the bark
of the branch on which you perch
perfect disguise
who would surmise
that you know nothing
of your wisdom?

No rain today
The clouds
Have gone away
Blue horizon
Sunshine pure
A lovely
Sunny day
Rise up
And join the fray.

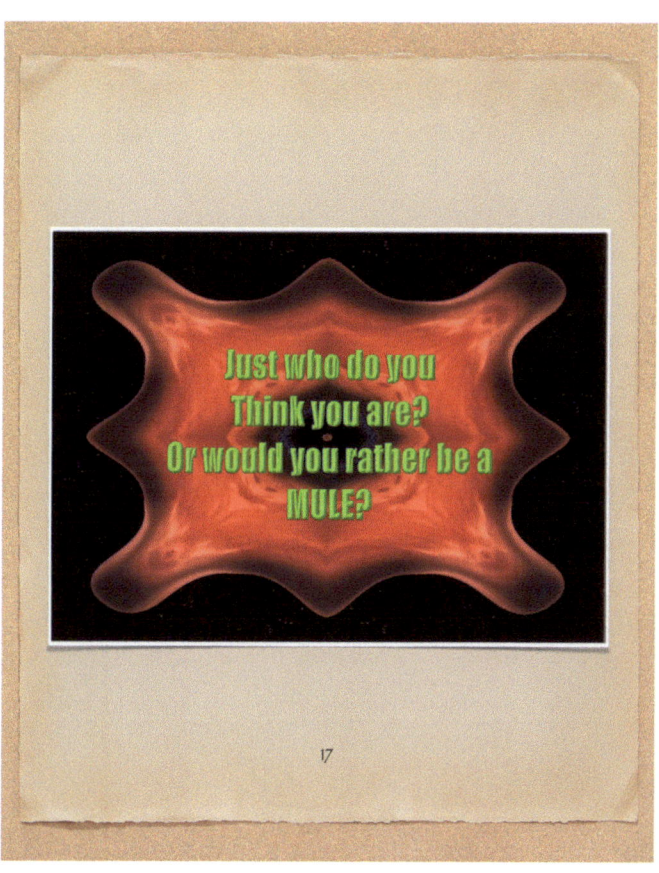

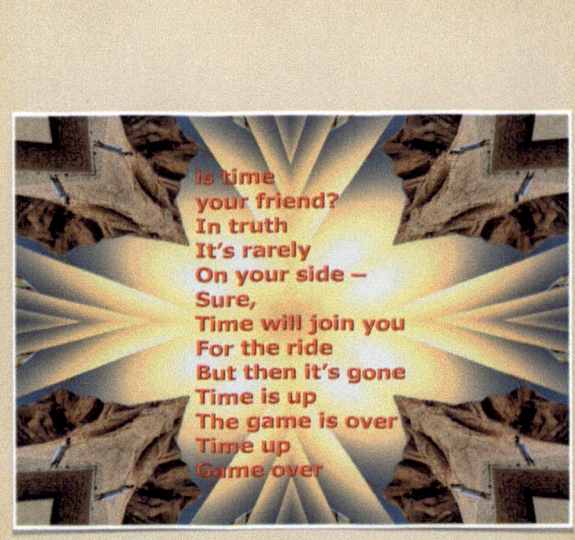

Is time
your friend?
In truth
It's rarely
On your side –
Sure,
Time will join you
For the ride
But then it's gone
Time is up
The game is over
Time up
Game over

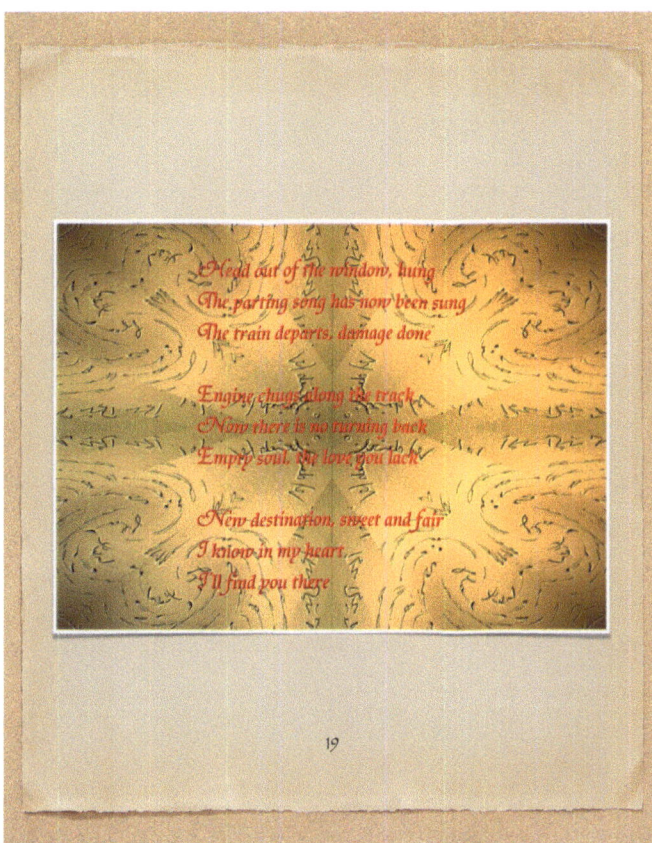

Head out of the window, hung
The parting song has now been sung
The train departs, damage done

Engine chugs along the track
Now there is no turning back
Empty soul, the love you lack

New destination, sweet and fair
I know in my heart
I'll find you there

19

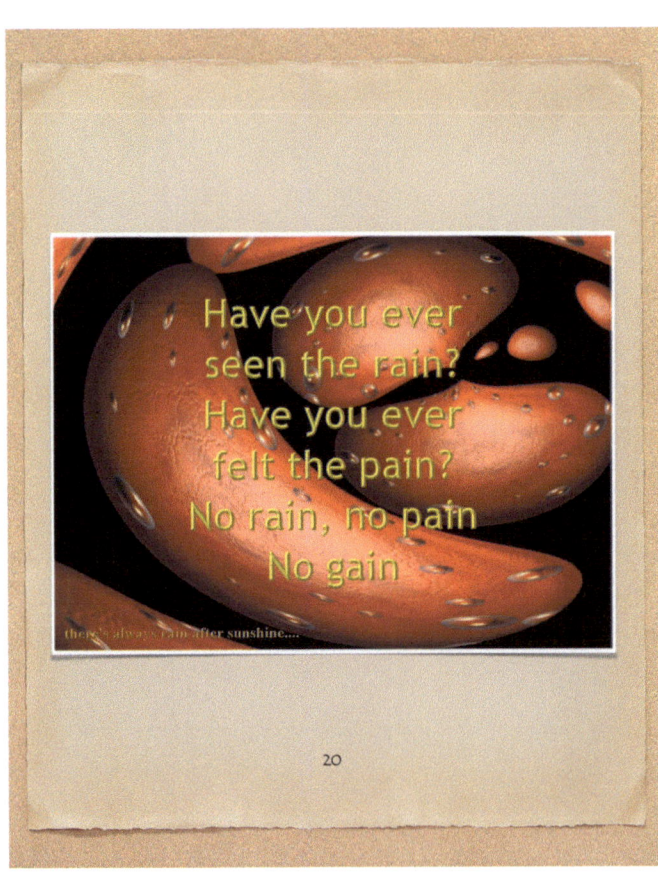

Have you ever
seen the rain?
Have you ever
felt the pain?
No rain, no pain
No gain

there's always rain after sunshine....

In a room full of light
someone started flicking switches
first subtle wobble, no alarm
and trembling hand, little harm
then fading eyes, no surprise
brain a maze, desperate cries
for help in the gathering darkness
switch after switch
flick after flick
the gloom descended.
Can *someone* turn the lights *back* on?

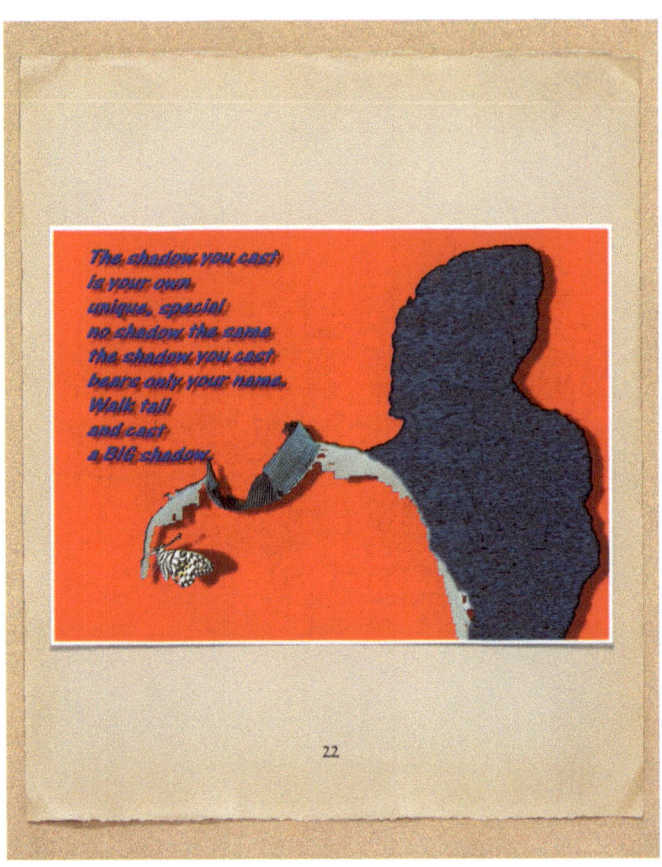

The shadow you cast
is your own,
unique, special,
no shadow the same
the shadow you cast
bears only your name.
Walk tall
and cast
a BIG shadow.

22

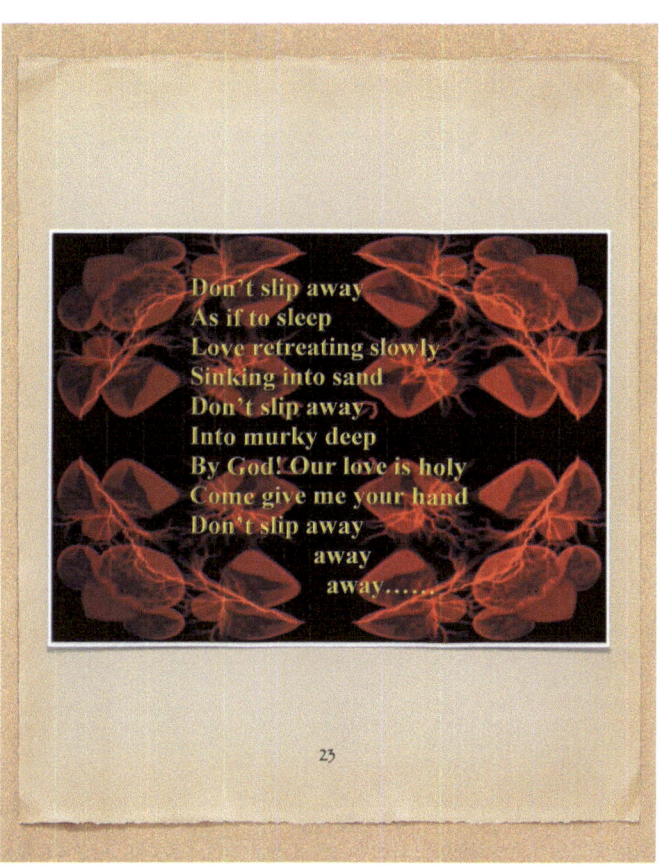

Don't slip away
As if to sleep
Love retreating slowly
Sinking into sand
Don't slip away
Into murky deep
By God! Our love is holy
Come give me your hand
Don't slip away
         away
            away......

23

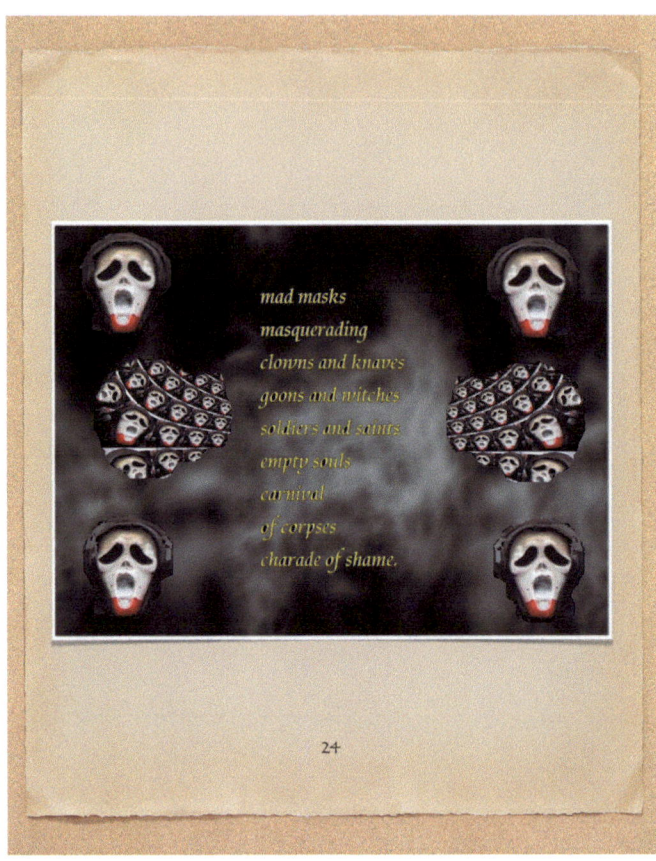

mad masks
masquerading
clowns and knaves
goons and witches
soldiers and saints
empty souls
carnival
of corpses
charade of shame.

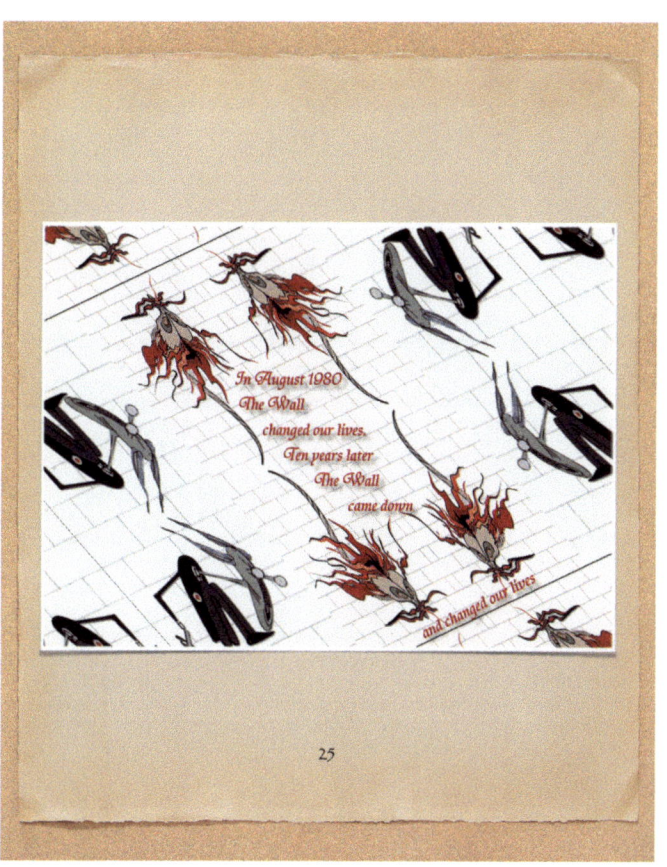

In August 1980
The Wall
changed our lives.
Ten years later
The Wall
came down

and changed our lives

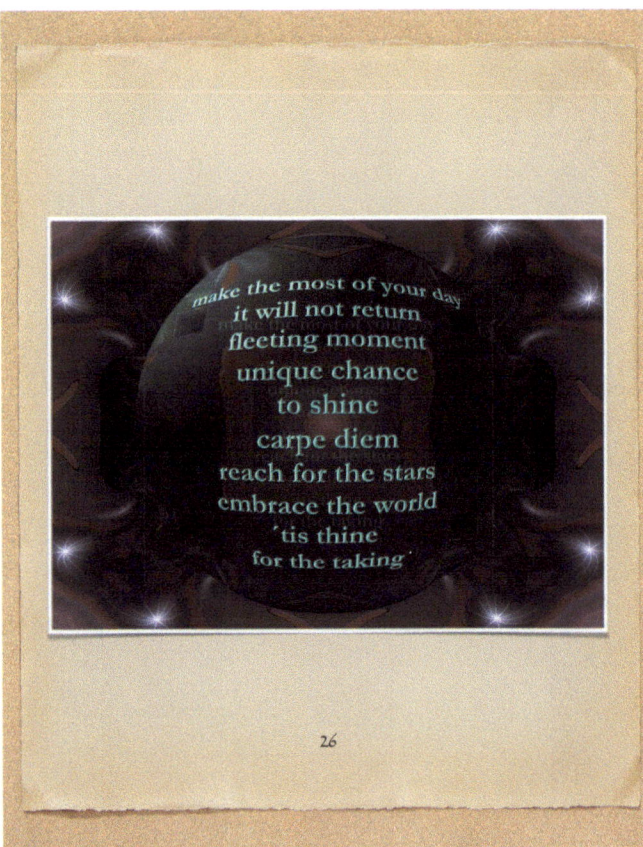

make the most of your day
it will not return
fleeting moment
unique chance
to shine
carpe diem
reach for the stars
embrace the world
'tis thine
for the taking

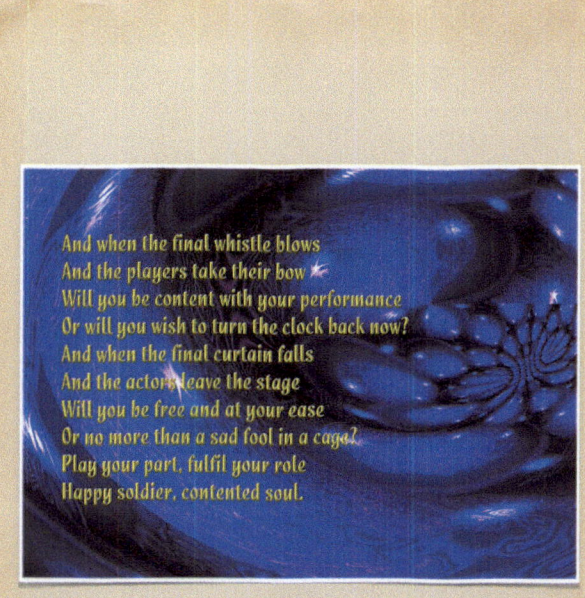

And when the final whistle blows
And the players take their bow
Will you be content with your performance
Or will you wish to turn the clock back now?
And when the final curtain falls
And the actors leave the stage
Will you be free and at your ease
Or no more than a sad fool in a cage?
Play your part, fulfil your role
Happy soldier, contented soul.

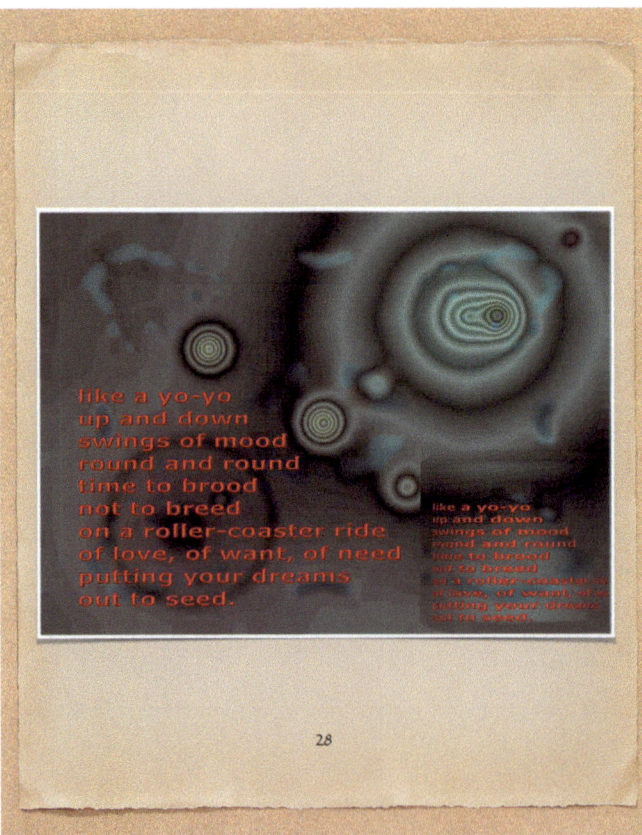

like a yo-yo
up and down
swings of mood
round and round
time to brood
not to breed
on a roller-coaster ride
of love, of want, of need
putting your dreams
out to seed.

like a yo-yo
up and down
swings of mood
round and round
time to brood
not to breed
on a roller-coaster ride
of love, of want, of need
putting your dreams
out to seed.

hurtling downhill
the bumpy road of life
lurching round corners
hidden bends
dark tunnels
blind exits
swirling through
uncharted waters
ALIVE!

29

Birdshit on my hat
Now what should we make of that?
They tell us that the world is round
I tend to think it's flat.

30

Watching the waves
Rolling ceaselessly to shore
Enduring ocean
Perpetual motion
Seagulls swoop forevermore.
Gazing at the sun
Sinking slowly in the west
Eternal sunlight
Infinite daylight
Tides that never rest.
Restless ocean
Tireless sea.

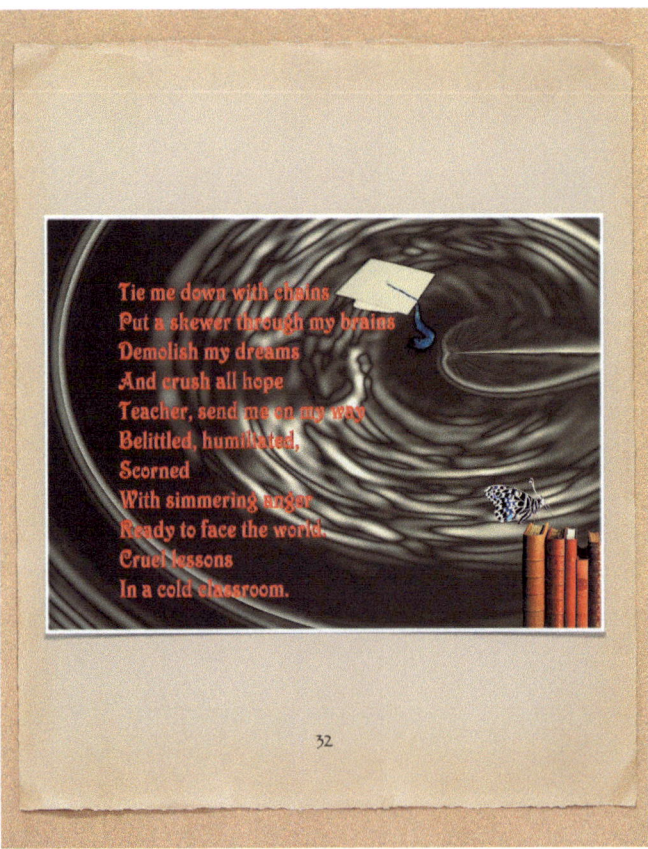

Tie me down with chains
Put a skewer through my brains
Demolish my dreams
And crush all hope
Teacher, send me on my way
Belittled, humiliated,
Scorned
With simmering anger
Ready to face the world.
Cruel lessons
In a cold classroom.

Envoys of gloom
Ambassadors of doom
Holding court
Within my room.
Cacophony of sound
Chaos all around
Nerves fraught
Mind run aground.

33

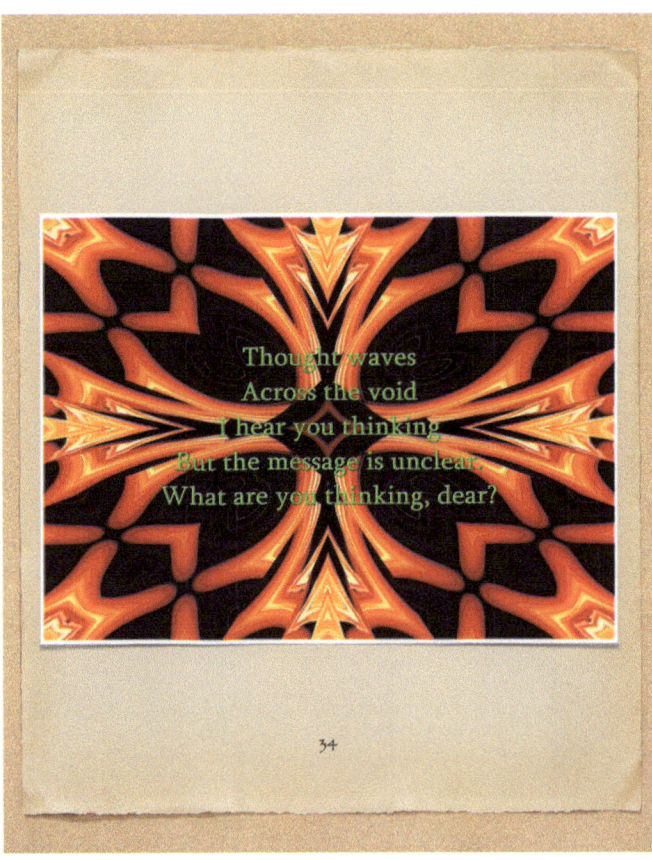

Thought waves
Across the void
I hear you thinking
But the message is unclear.
What are you thinking, dear?

34

The ball rolls
Our lucky numbers
Scream out for attention
But as usual
The ball rolls by.
Paradise lost again

35

magic stones
sent to protect you
their colours
breathing all the secrets
of life
stone charms
to keep you out of harm's
way.

tears swell
so powerless to help
eyes to the sky
in agnostic prayer
that someone
will place a
protecting hand
over you.

37

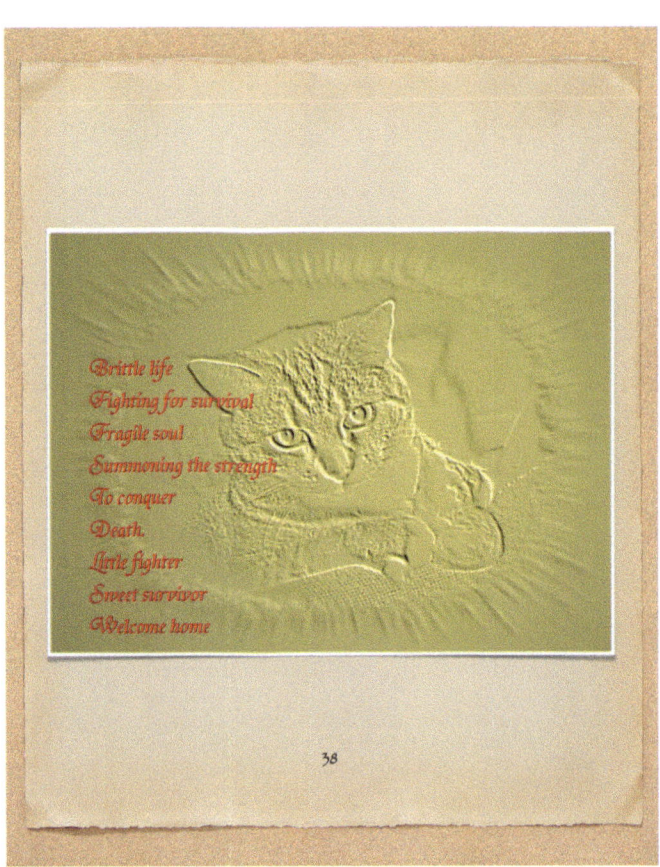

Brittle life
Fighting for survival
Fragile soul
Summoning the strength
To conquer
Death.
Little fighter
Sweet survivor
Welcome home

38

each intricate tiny flower
upon the hillside
catches but a
brief glimpse of life
and treats us
to its beauty
for a mere
blink of the eye.
each tiny flower

39

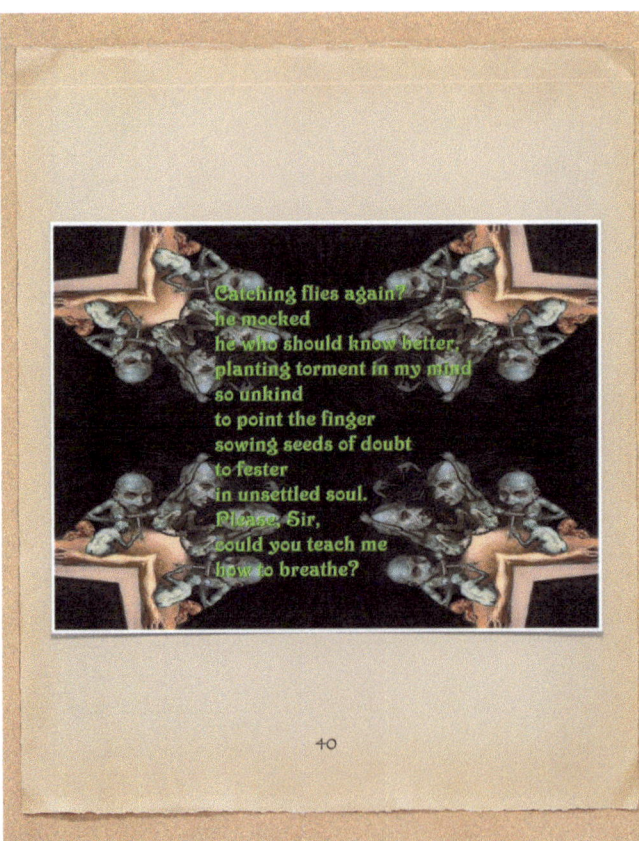

Catching flies again?
he mocked
he who should know better,
planting torment in my mind
so unkind
to point the finger
sowing seeds of doubt
to fester
in unsettled soul.
Please, Sir,
could you teach me
how to breathe?

40

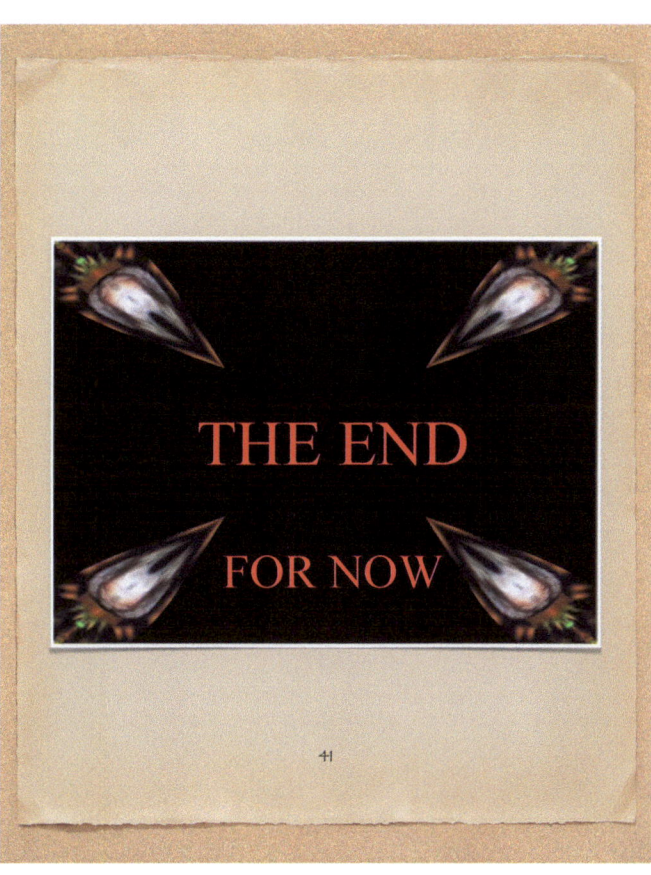

41